Rabbits

by Mari Schuh

Consulting Editor: Gail Saunders-Smith, PhD

CAPSTONE PRESS
a capstone imprint

Pebble Plus is published by Capstone Press,
1710 Roe Crest Drive, North Mankato, Minnesota 56003
www.capstonepub.com

Library of Congress Cataloging-in-Publication Data
Schuh, Mari C., 1975–
  Rabbits / by Mari Schuh.
pages cm. — (Pebble plus. Backyard animals)
Summary: "An introduction to rabbits, their characteristics, habitat, food, life cycle, and threats. Includes a hands-on activity related to wildlife watching"— Provided by publisher.
  Audience: Ages 4–8.
  Audience: K to grade 3.
  Includes bibliographical references and index.
ISBN 978-1-4914-2086-7 (library binding) — ISBN 978-1-4914-2327-1 (ebook PDF)
  1. Rabbits—Juvenile literature. I. Title.
  QL737.L32S386 2015
  599.32—dc23   2014032328

Editorial Credits
Nikki Bruno Clapper, editor; Juliette Peters, designer;
Tracy Cummins, media researcher; Tori Abraham, production specialist

The author dedicates this book to her beloved rabbits, Karma and Kindle.

Photo Credits
iStockphotos: ElementalImaging, 24, Natural_Warp, 22 Left; Shutterstock: Bruce MacQueen, 21, Chris Vennix, 17 Background, Denise Kappa, 1, DL Pohl, 5, GGRIGOROV, 13, HHsu, 15, Ingrid Curry, 19, Leena Robinson, Cover, Lorraine Hudgins, 22 Right, Paginar, Back Cover, PinkPueblo, Design Element, Pressmaster, 11, Steve Heap, Design Element, Cover Design Element; Thinkstock: Giorgio Perbellini, 7, Leoba, 9, Nick Biemans, 17

Note to Parents and Teachers

The Backyard Animals set supports national curriculum standards for science related to life science and ecosystems. This book describes and illustrates rabbits. The images support early readers in understanding the text. The repetition of words and phrases helps early readers learn new words. This book also introduces early readers to subject-specific vocabulary words, which are defined in the Glossary section. Early readers may need assistance to read some words and to use the Table of Contents, Glossary, Read More, Internet Sites, Critical Thinking Using the Common Core, and Index sections of the book.

Printed in the United States of America in Stevens Point, Wisconsin.
092014   008479WZS15

Table of Contents

Backyard Rabbits

A furry face peeks from around a fence. A long ear tilts to hear a noise. The animal hops away. A rabbit lives in your backyard!

Rabbits are mammals.
They have fur and feed milk
to their young. Wild rabbits
weigh 2 to 5 pounds
(1 to 2.3 kilograms).

Rabbits have long ears and back legs. A rabbit's ears help it hear danger far away. Strong back legs help the rabbit hop quickly.

Rabbits can stand in one spot and see all around their bodies. They can even see what is behind and above them.

Backyard rabbits live
in bushes and tall grass.
They make shallow nests.
They also hide in
underground burrows.

What Rabbits Do

Female rabbits make
soft nests for their young.
They line the nests with fur.
Females give birth to
four to six kits.

Kits grow quickly. They live on their own after three to six weeks. Most wild rabbits live for one to two years.

Rabbits in the Garden

Rabbits visit backyard gardens. They eat vegetables and other plants. If a rabbit visits your yard, do not go near the animal.

Try planting clover near your other plants. Rabbits might eat the clover instead of your garden plants. Watch the rabbits nibble and chew!

Hands-On Activity: Rabbit Journal

Do rabbits live in your neighborhood? Look for some clues. Write down what you find in a notebook. Here are some things to look for.

Look for rabbit tracks on the ground.
Rabbit tracks look like this: ⟶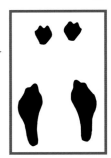
Rabbits eat tree bark in winter.
Look for patches of chewed bark near the bottom of tree trunks.
Do you see any holes in your yard?
Some rabbits hide in underground burrows.

Glossary

burrow—a hole or tunnel in the ground made or used by an animal

clover—small, leafy plants that grow low to the ground

kit—a baby rabbit

mammal—a warm-blooded animal with hair or fur; female mammals feed milk to their young.

shallow—not deep

tracks—marks left behind by a person or animal

Read More

Jordan, Apple. *Guess Who Hops.* Bookworms: Guess Who. New York: Marshall Cavendish Benchmark, 2012.

Marsico, Katie. *Rabbits.* Community Connections: How Do We Live Together? Ann Arbor, Mich.: Cherry Lake Pub., 2010.

Zobel, Derek. *Rabbits.* Blastoff! Readers: Backyard Wildlife. Minneapolis: Bellwether Media, 2011.

Internet Sites

FactHound offers a safe, fun way to find Internet sites related to this book. All of the sites on FactHound have been researched by our staff.

Here's all you do:

Visit *www.facthound.com*

Type in this code: 9781491420867

Super-cool stuff!

Check out projects, games and lots more at
www.capstonekids.com

Critical Thinking
Using the Common Core

1. Why are a rabbit's long ears helpful? (Key Ideas and Details)

2. What is a burrow? How does a rabbit make its burrow comfortable? (Craft and Structure)

Index

Word Count: 202
Grade: 1
Early-Intervention Level: 18

24